THE MYSTERY OF HALLOWEEN

Coloring Book for Relaxation and Meditation

Catherine Johnson

THE MYSTERY OF HALLOWEEN

Coloring Book for Relaxation and Meditation

Copyright: Published in the United States by Catherine Johnson
Published October 2016

ISBN-13: 978-1539846390

ISBN-10: 1539846393

HAPPY HALLOWEEN

Thank you

www.ingramcontent.com/pod-product-compliance
Lightning Source LLC
Chambersburg PA
CBHW051950280526
45789CB00009B/3236